Derivative of the Moving Image

Derivative of the Moving Image

Jennifer Bartlett

University of New Mexico Press | Albuquerque

12 11 10 09 08 07   1 2 3 4 5 6 7

Library of Congress Cataloging-in-Publication Data

Bartlett, Jennifer, 1969–
    Derivative of the moving image / Jennifer Bartlett.
        p. cm. — (Mary Burritt Christiansen poetry series)
    ISBN 978-0-8263-4133-4 (cloth : alk. paper)
    I. Title.
    PS3602.A83953D47 2007
    811'.6—dc22
                                2007022079

These poems first appeared in the following,
to whose editors I am grateful: *Ash Canyon Review,*
Blue Mesa Review, Bughouse, First Intensity, How2,
In Company: An Anthology of New Mexico Poets
after 1960, Psalm 151, Ratapallax, smallspiralnotebook,
The Boston Globe, and *Women's Studies Quarterly.*

Book and cover design and type composition by
Kathleen Sparkes. This book is typeset using
Utopia 10.5/14.5. The display type is Frutiger Light.

Mary Burritt Christiansen
Poetry Series
V. B. Price, Series Editor

Also available in the
University of New Mexico Press
Mary Burritt Christiansen Poetry Series:

Poets of the Non-Existent City:
    Los Angeles in the McCarthy Era
    edited by Estelle Gershgoren Novak

Selected Poems of Gabriela Mistral
    edited by Ursula K. Le Guin

Deeply Dug In by R. L. Barth

Amulet Songs: Poems Selected and New by Lucile Adler

In Company: An Anthology of New Mexico Poets After
    1960 edited by Lee Bartlett, V. B. Price, and
    Dianne Edenfield Edwards

Tiempos Lejanos: Poetic Images from the Past
    by Nasario García

Refuge of Whirling Light by Mary Beath

The River Is Wide/El río es ancho:
    Twenty Mexican Poets, a Bilingual Anthology
    edited and translated by Marlon L. Fick

A Scar Upon Our Voice by Robin Coffee

CrashBoomLove: A Novel in Verse by Juan Felipe Herrera

In a Dybbuk's Raincoat: Collected Poems by Bert Meyers

Rebirth of Wonder: Poems of the Common Life
    by David M. Johnson

Broken and Reset: Selected Poems, 1966 to 2006
    by V. B. Price

The Curvature of the Earth by Gene Frumkin and
    Alvaro Cardona-Hine

for emma, for jim, and mostly, for jeff

Contents

The Music Of:

Hypnagogic Diary

Foreword

A work translucent with humane insight and the candor of reality as a metaphor for grace, *Derivative of the Moving Image* is New Mexico native Jennifer Bartlett's first book of poems. And I am sure there will be a great many more. Bartlett is a poet of unique and startling gifts, one whose moxie, integrity, and wit bring to the reader poems wide awake with confidence and amazement.

Her poems deal, in part, with the crushing circumstances of untimely and unexpected deaths in her family and of the emotional traumas and physical limitations that afflict us all from time to time. But these poems are in no sense morbid or depressing. Their stunning metaphors and intriguingly oblique, though telling, narratives are often autobiographical and, at the same time, accessible in a universal way. They embody an intense and even inspiring awareness of what it takes to survive and prevail over horrendous misfortunes and long runs of bad luck. Writing from complex life situations, Bartlett's work communicates on an uncanny personal level with a wide variety of readers. Some of her poems are so honest and idiosyncratic that they give the feeling of having overheard a conversation. Other poems seem to solve riddles and conundrums of personal growth and give the reader a sense of being the recipient of an unexpected correspondence that comes exactly at the right time. The intensity of her metaphors, the iridescence of her humor, the generosity of her openness, make Jennifer Bartlett's poems overflow with a joyousness that nothing can thwart.

Jennifer Bartlett was born in northern California, raised in Albuquerque, New Mexico, and received her undergraduate degree at the University of New Mexico and an MFA in Creative Writing from Vermont College. Not long ago at a reading in which I took part, I witnessed her draw a crowd to rapt attention as she read her work. Her reputation as a reader, both in New Mexico and New York, attests to the magical quality she has onstage. In New York, Bartlett served as arts editor and staff writer for *WE Magazine,* an internationally regarded journal dedicated to issues concerning the disabled. Bartlett was *WE*'s first full-time writer/editor to have cerebral palsy. Along with her husband, the writer Jim Stewart, she is cofounder and editor of Saint Elizabeth Street Press and its literary journal. In 1996, she received the Bruce P. Rossley Literary New Voices Award in Boston. A year before she received the Zora Neale Hurston Award, a grant to attend the summer writing program at the Naropa Institute. In 2005, she won a prestigious New York Foundation for the Arts poetry fellowship.

The late poet and patron Mary Burritt Christansen endowed UNM Press's poetry series to support the work of "unestablished" but stellar poets at the beginning of their careers. Jennifer Bartlett brings to the Christansen poetry collection a voice of the future, one that is already mature and grounded in political savvy, compelling in its aesthetic curiosity and daring, and fully aware of the intricate social and psychological challenges that lay ahead for us all in a world of rapid and often bewildering change.

—V. B. Price
Albuquerque

Acknowledgments

A special thank you to my mentors and teachers:
Lee Bartlett, Nathaniel Tarn, Gene Frumkin,
Bill Olsen, Betsy Sholl, David Rivard, Mary Rueffle,
Mary Power, Edwin Torres, V. B. Price, and Janet
Rodney. Also, thank you to Roxann Beck-Foley,
Michael Foley, Aneta, Al Bartlett, and Barbara
Beck. Finally, my dear lifelong friends: Eric, Rachel,
Deanna, Tomas, Dion, Peter, Jeff, Julia, and Tara.

When I Got My First Tattoo I Was.

From a Paris Hotel Room

It was the spring after my sister died that I began to notice the moths. They would follow me from room to room beating against the window shades or showing themselves in the one tiny patch of light as I dressed for the day. Some days, some hours, I would count as many as twenty and still they held no significance for me. I saw them as many see the trees that line the highway, just passing objects.

One afternoon when the rains came I let the girls take off all their clothes and run naked in the yard while I danced around them in my blue nanny dress. I don't know why I did that. That night the moths were so large that they woke me like a burglar might. I put bowls of sugar around the house to keep them from the books.

Occasionally, the elder of the two girls will touch my arm and speak of my sister as if she remembers her. She tells me that my sister is dead.

Then the moths. They like to linger in hot places like the roof of the car. The smaller ones cling to my hands as I water the garden in the morning. When I ask others if they notice the creatures with the same consistency most deny it or act as though it is ordinary. The few that show an interest describe them as hideous monsters. I argue them to be more beautiful than butterflies.

Coup de Grace

I am on dreamtime. Everything is played out in my bed first
around the curves of sleep. Angels lie with me against these
worn sheets, assuring my journey. I tiptoe. There is a yellow
box of razors on top of the refrigerator, happier than the knives
that lie dormant in the closed drawer. I reach through dust to
find them. And here's what my mind looks like: a tiny image of
water or an empty hand. I asked for a road map and was given
silver blades, translucent thoughts, and a red body. I start at
my ankles, going further than what time or drama will allow.
I am only the space between each vein. And here's what my
hallway looks like: white walls that call for insanity and a plain
wood floor. There is a light at either end and people pull in
and out like trains constantly beginning a long voyage. I run
to follow them but only glimpse their backs.

M. is the one who finds me. At first instinct he collapses to
his knees, his lips at the base of my feet as if these sucking
motions can save me. He unpins a note from my dress. It says,
Do not disturb or *I wanted to end before the world did.* I can
feel his hand at the back of my neck and a mouth full of blood
screaming my name. I, wordless, rage to tell him, *Let me go!
Let me go! My sister is waiting in the bed we shared as children
and her arms are open.* Not knowing what to do he takes me
out into the air and lays me against the dying grass. This is
where we begin to give up, the both of us.

Ghost Boy

I think about death all the time now. She slides her body
between us, even on the most vivid days. We are as simple as
this, moving through rain, your thin hands reaching for fireflies
to save them from the heat. Why do you desert me? You know
my limbs are fragile; like paper dolls I could tear at any second.
I cannot bear one moment without your eyes in my direction,
your breath writing notes across my skin. Or: lying across water
we face opposite directions. I am the drop of a hat on your bed.
Blue, I think it was.

When I Got My First Tattoo I Was.

(You will say)

You will say that I am stupid for telling this. I am stupid and no one is interested. And I will say that I don't care because we are like that. And I. I saw an old girlfriend of yours standing in the street today. Like you standing in the dark, always, always, just standing. Your house smelling like tattoo ink, if it can have a smell. And that's where it all begins, with this smell, this smell.

(With her grabbing at my feet)

With her grabbing at my feet we swam the length of the pool, the sun beating our skin red. I went into the laundry room to take off my wet dress, stood there naked. She wanted to get a tattoo once. A dragon, I think it was, down her arm or across a thigh maybe. But she stopped and we stood outside the car. She put her lips to my neck like a mother might. She told me that this fantasy would only bring disaster.

(No one wants to hear about my dead sister)

No one wants to hear about my dead sister and her arms or the distant lack of them. Her one collapsing lung thrown onto the emergency room floor. The doctor with the glasses just steps over it. It is common, these strewn body parts. When the dead are brought up in conversation they shatter on the tile like broken stones; the mention of my sister makes their ears burn until they fall off, ashes. No one wants to hear about my dead sister, but in this age of body scarification everyone dreams of stories of ink running down legs or arms, even with these razors.

(You have to understand my first tattoo)

You have to understand my first tattoo, my first. Once you make the decision there is no returning. Having the needle at your skin becomes an obsession that you play out again and again. And me. Me shaking as I wait in your apartment one hour before my appointment. I settle into his chair, my arms dreaming of lead. I am nervous and scattered like the stars. *Are you sure you want it?* Once the decision is made there is no returning. I smile like a masochist. He digs the needle into my skin. And he is grasping at my shaking elbow. When he removes his fingers there are red marks and people drift in and out of this house. He continues to draw.

(And now I)

Now, I make my way across these landscapes, this girl gone from my near breath. Still, somehow, she is always near fixing things broken by my footsteps, her letters scrolled across my skin. Even in the best of dreams this ink disappearing makes me despair but she gives my painted limbs rest.

Tulip Farm

I am going to Seattle, she said, as if trying to recreate herself. In her language it seemed like two words, as if she were going to see someone, not just a place, treed and wet. He told her to bring a jacket. He told her even though it was summer, it was cold and his arms wouldn't be enough to keep her.

I picked the longest skirt, the one that would tell me how to walk like a woman but the grass was wet and the skirt wept. When I was young I couldn't remember what sorrow was, this gentle ache of bones. Night meant sneaking out into the yard to watch owls or sleeping to fireworks from a nearby baseball field. If thoughts are only symbols of memories is it appropriate then that you think in notes and I in despair?

She was a sure thing, an infallible bet. Even the fastest of animals sometimes collapse. It's in the abstract motion of the legs, not something that happens fast: the act of falling in love, the letting of blood into the water, trying to keep things clean.

Elegy for the Trees

The two children stumble onto a dirt road. A tractor drags a
dying horse into the frame, leaving it there. The girl reaches for
its cold back. "He's dying." Her brother, the smaller of the two,
begins to cry. Noise from a wedding startles the background.
The bride emerges, her hysterical young husband rushing
behind her. The wind picks at her veil, the wedding party
trailing after, joyous, drunk. "He's dead."

Tom wrote to you every day, forgetting the irony of paper,
nature's graphic language. He destroyed all of his writings,
as if ideas were flammable or would not float on water.
His presence was like that, a burning.

Certain Northwestern tribes believe that when a tree is
cut down one must look away as it falls or its soul will die.
That is why, for them, lumberjacking is considered a form
of madness.

That is why the moment my sister left her body our parents
made us turn from her. My mother and I had a similar dream
that night. My sister stood in the tree near our house speaking
her arboreal language. We were unable to translate.

The children accept a ride with a stranger. While the boy
sleeps the stranger pulls the girl into the back of his truck.
We do not see this. We see the boy forming his sister's name
in sleep's frantic alphabet. We see the stranger adjust his
clothes, the blood on her hand.

Tom's wife could have been Radnóti's wife through sifting
bodies in order to find his poems. By the time she rescued
Tom's autobiography from the fire it was one page long.
In a manuscript of a hundred words he used "tree" twenty-
seven times, this or a variation.

Logistically, you argue, there is little chance the children
survive the passage across the river. The bullets obscured by
the mist must find the softest parts of the girl. The tree that
they hold in their arms when they reach the other side is not
really their father but a symbol of.

Derivative of the Moving Image

Derivative of the Moving Image

She is a cliché as in a story told
over and over caught in the telling or
a negative waiting to be turned into an image,
a visual diary, the thing that catches the eye.
It could be anything that traps you,
the color of her scarf, the swinging of her dress,
          that makes you think it is fate,
holds you there, keeping you at my arm's length.

Last night, alone at the movies, waiting for the light to open,
          to tell its particular reality against
the white background,
I turned around to accidentally observe
the ultimate act of intimacy, two boys kissing
          just briefly,
risking everything or nothing by it
          in a supposedly forbidden gesture.
But I guess we should give up trying to guess
          the exact intentions of others.

For example, we think of her hands differently—
          distance versus song—
while still referring to them as hands. It could be any
part of the body, so vast I can't think to name them all;
          even you are not just the words
I use to describe you, not the sum of them.

Trapped in a history of watching,
          waiting for the image to rush
    you want the dialogue to be minimal,
describe yourself as silent in halted speech
          fading further into yourself, becoming
so small I can barely make you out
          through your vanishing act.
If speech for you means merely breaking apart space
          you are there, already broken.

Outside, the buds contrive their upward mobility.
Soon the apartment will be trapped in leaves.
I can hear them each morning, crows outside the bathroom window
                building a nest in the highest branches,
their presence neither romantic nor comforting but
                a gross distraction
as they jump up and down, talking a mile a minute,
                tree limbs scraping the side of the house.
I imagine them to be mice hidden between
                wall and sink
                    hollowing out the walls,
forming a new landscape within this predetermined one—
what would be your study if only you'd stayed to unpack your things.

The scratching is like the timetable in a train station,
                clicking over, endlessly changing its mind,
beating its wings into plate glass.
I would go two thousand miles just to run into you
and I did, scarred from the motion of three days of train,
I waited for you beneath this metallic bird,
                everything not still,
but rather a constant product of movement
like a body of water that can't quite merge with land
                but keeps at its attempt
                    consistently hammering the surface.
We spoke later about how strange it was,
                a sort of blind date
for two people who knew each other implicitly,
                my voice no longer a disembodied telephone lyric.
But that kind of awkward passion,
                that strangeness, is not
the kind you are thinking of now,
                but rather *tout nouveau, tout beau.*

Of course, I wish I had done it differently when I saw you with her,
                but then again *hysteria is the soul voyaging.*

Instead of coldly leaving to wander the vegetable aisle,
                    I stayed, flaying sound like a target,
trying to bring you back into this world. Rain is so
difficult to capture on film, no matter how you light it.
It was as though we had to walk through
                              the scene again and again
                                        in altering gradations
until you found the right movement,
                                   the right way to get it down.
                    The girl took instant flight
or perhaps it was you who sent her away,
                         crossing the street toward me.
Without greetings we fought,
                        eddying in the alit
green of the grocery store awning,
          a backdrop for domesticity;
                         that certain, obvious kind of ending.

Camera Obscura

Birds lift from the surface.

Now, only a few swimmers remain,
their bodies black fragments
diving into the froth, forcing the still air.

At the edge a dog hesitates,
his owner turning outward
as the sea gathers its endless body.

Light pulls the tide
in and out
of your palm.
The light needs this movement, us
looking down into it like spectrographs.

When I was a child
my parents brought me here
but kept me outside,
excluded from this dark chamber,
the projected landscape.

Words were never my own.

Now, sometimes when I speak
my voice is a pinhole. By the time
an image reaches the surface
it is hazed, blurred, never reflecting
quite what I mean to say.

We're alone, you say.

Then—

Let's make love, raising your knee,
climbing into the water.

A Man and a Woman Standing in the
Rain in Front of a Candy Store

You know I'm thinking about China again,
about women who live under tents of long black hair,
how their skin might feel under certain amounts of pressure.
Your gaze follows me to the doorstep, drops itself there.

How can I tell you what your hands are
but two instruments of song,
notes that you hide behind like a child playing hide-and-go-seek.
You are the sum of these secrets not telling themselves always,
only when necessary.

Or:

How can I tell you what your hands mean to me,
the brushing of them over tabletops,
over my shoulders, leading to the rest of my body.

Words are stones that we pick up on the walk along the way.
I save your words like keepsakes locked in a box
pushed far under the bed.
I will take them out when your voice
has long sung itself to sleep,
when your shallow breath has given itself to another.
I plan on your leaving.

I can't make your skin my own,
nor your heart my heart,
knowing this we dance around each other
encircled in the smallness of our laughter,
you lean toward me when we walk
as if this leaning will save you from your fear of the world.

The two hundredth question asks:
does your soul ever leave your body?
Yes, often.
For example, the night my sister died
and we left the hospital together.
For example, the time your wrist touched my dress
and I imagined its keeping itself there.
I am susceptible to angels.

I want to show you how buildings can fold into themselves.
The park is getting cooler now,
the musicians linger over their last notes.
One day when I am older and you are happier
we will go on this walk like my sisters
when they chased their shadows around the Bordeaux courtyard,
once around.

Li Po's

In a few months you will consider
leaving me for someone else,
tired of our daily alphabet,
my compulsion to drag language
kicking and screaming
toward that which it most resists.
Then you will decide that
sometimes, often,
the best action is no action.

Tonight, we sit in North Beach
wrapped around our rum and cokes
with your friend Jim and his wife,
me, trying to make sense of the groove,
the repeat in
your broken record of a heart,
the crack and sweep
of dice in the background,
the players' maniacal voices competing
with disco music droning its one note
like a drowning insect some
cruel child has pulled the wings from.
I am the only one touched by the strangeness
of it, the awkwardness of
the young kids, the Chinese men,
patriots almost, bent toward their illegality.

Jim describes a sculpture
of his parents, a portrait of each,
the thing clouding itself
over an image of his mother,

then father, then mother,
like an impatient lover
pressed to the window, fogging the glass.
his meandering heartbeat and breath regulate
the distortion, the equation between them.

I am in love with him
only because he is so much like you,
a man likely to fall into a river
trying to embrace the moon.

As we leave the bar, I turn back
toward the shrine for Li Po,
colored lights illuminating the orange
crate, candlelight licking
the supposed image of him
over and over.
I am only able to glance at it
before we are back on the emptied street
in the neighborhood of now-gone poets.

Tomorrow we will fly east
against the current of my familiar
through the darkening landscape,
our images projected toward each other but
never quite meeting,
a series of distractions veiling the light,
creating the distance between us. Always
practicing good-byes, I am getting good
in this practicing.

Reading Hannah Arendt in Spanish Harlem

He wanted to know the method of light,
the way the directness of it
fades into shadow. Then, he felt
he could attribute an explanation to anything.
That evening, I point out,
There is a marching band outside.
You say, *No, I think it is the ice cream truck*
that comes to sell after twelve o'clock
on a Sunday.
You are turned away putting on
some/*a kind of blue.*
The two surfaces of music compete with each other
but the din of this falling is so loud
we can hardly hear anything over it.

And Arendt? How do we explain her contradictions?
Although she loved him, surely she must
have realized his anti-Semitism, his activities.
Perhaps this is how she learned the truth about love,
not what Akhmatova claimed it to be—
something that makes one *sick all the time*—
but rather, a sort of denial, an overlooking.
Yet, when two people add it up
it turns out that they, more often than not,
were at the same place at the same time.

Outside the truck has turned the corner
erasing its own tepid sound;
from this vantage point the city presents itself
as a mere series of lights;
from this vantage point.

Going to Yugoslavia

After,
we stood outside the bar, the four of us,
her husband Dusan lagging behind,
his monologue unfolding
like film feeding its endless body
                        through light.
Your life too is like this—
                the deluge of frames
a significant, constant humming, me
            (in the foreground)
trying to marry image to image,
                pushing
to make sense of the thing.

When we parted, even though
we had already said good-bye,
we turned back toward her,
                the distance making
her look smaller, more comforting,
                than ever.

Before leaving she reiterated the story,
wire stretching from nursing home
to spire reaching the cathedral,
placed here, high above Amsterdam Avenue,
the tightrope artist waited in a
                hurry and delay,
the look on his face so intense
                        as if it
were this intensity holding him,
                keeping him midair.

With the crowd threatening to pull him under
           he descended wingless
believing that, in order to create beauty, one must
risk one's entire life, recognize the invisible,
the line threading person to person, thus
           even when she leaves, she will remain;
us, like him, trying to do this without nets.

On Assayas's *L'eau Froide*

We disagreed on the film's ending
as she stood naked
unaffected by the fictional

unbearable cold;
after she slid her ghost
of a body from him.

When he awoke he found a note
near the river
folded underneath her clothes.

He turned it over and over
to show us, the viewers, and himself,
that the paper was blank.

I, in all my practicality,
exclaimed it was because
she did not have a pen,

while you, always the romantic, took the absence
to mean that there was nothing to say.
Both of us turning, as usual,

in different directions
only to arrive at the same place.

But today is the fifth day
of spring and, finally,
my thin dresses
have righted themselves.

If you don't know it
I'll tell you, how the body
reacts to weather creating

the kind of nostalgia you speak of
and the air speaks its particular grammar.

Finally, you tell yourself, a season without longing.

Essays on Birds and Light

Ornithology

Being disabled is not what you think.
Limitation exists only within the context of others
as the only language the body knows
is that which it tells itself.
Movement appears painful from a distance
when rather it is just the body reiterating itself.
Like one of da Vinci's hopelessly grounded things
these limbs make a contortionist out of me,
lifting my one good wing from the sidewalk
I unfold finally, cinematically,
after a winter of wordless birds.

(in)Retrospect

In an attempt to accomplish emptiness, or her attempt
      to re-inscribe space,
she might climb on the roof to sell mornings (mournings)
represented by fragmented glass. They were more or
      less expensive
depending on time of day, depending on how far they
      progressed into winter,
the ones right before Christmas being the most expensive.

She writes, "Dear George, feel free to use this to pay for
      your hospital bills
as needed. Instructions and price list included."
      She writes *dear.*

In the room of halves, there is a white telephone against the
      wall with a note
saying if the telephone rings, pick it up and speak to the artist.
      We fall for it
hook, line, and sinker, wanting to wait there all day, but it is
the waiting, not the speaking that is the thing.

She *writes.*

It is said that every few days someone comes to clear the debris
from the garden. It is said that she cannot bring herself to
      throw it away.

(In the next room) you are counting our sorrows and
      happinesses as marked
by piles of stones and even when we add it all up, even when
      we consider Elizabeth,
Emma, Steve, Suzanne and the rest, our pile of happinesses
      is still larger.

(In the next room) she invites people to come cut away the
     remaining clothing
as she sits quietly onstage with an audience more than happy to
take place in the metaphor.

(In the next room) her husband sings *give peace a chance.*

Can a space be altered merely by language? For example,
     if I told
you this (small) room were larger would you believe me?
     If I told you this (square) room
were a circle, would you believe me? If I told you this
     (white) room
were blue would you believe me?
                              This white (or blue) room
described in blue (or white) ink so small it can barely make
     itself out.

We walk past the Dakota on our way to Dallas Barbeque as a way
     of defining
what space should look like, comparing her space to our own.
At first it was an obsession but
                              the novelty has worn off.
                              By the way, how much
should one be allowed to take up of any one place in the world?

She seems to want to re-describe space, but instead creates
     an emptiness.
Ordinary objects no longer have their previous identity but
are something that must remain untouched.

I will leave the poem in the garden with the others to up
     the chances
that she might see it, should this,
          in her list of urban myths, be true.

The Yellow One

In the wet New England spring we trekked up the hill
        to hear the Dalai Lama speak,
the getting there a pilgrimage in itself
much like the one taken each year in New Mexico
seventeen miles from desert
             to piñon grove into the village
with twin churches. This procession led into
the larger church with its collage of abandoned crutches
suspended over a hole of healing dirt that
            (a miracle in itself)
              replenished each day.
When William Everson came here he ate the dirt,
      this obscure, drastic gesture
leading him closer to God in that instant
          than all poems.

Now, Peter's friend's son lags behind,
        finding a pile of deadened sticks,
when told to pick, he chooses *the yellow one.*
Inside we witness it, the only sun for days
          trapped in the set design,
the center an obvious light blue,
        yellow jetting out in every direction
like light trying to escape. The Dalai Lama
stands in the middle giving his speech,
      guards surrounding him,
        holding on for dear life
to the corporeal, that which he does and does not need.
Even he confesses that compassion
      is not the most natural state of being.

Ten years ago, I sat in a room of Asian artifacts,
a scattering of Buddhist icons,
      the walls painted in gradations
                of white and gray
inventing a mountainous landscape
       that appeared lit from within.
The statues all seemed to be smiling,
one hand pressed forward, the other held as a lotus,
       content with any form of loss,
their quiet presence almost a cure for my own wordlessness.
They were not unlike Rublev's *Virgin of Vladamir*
that I saw once in a book but
     mother and child
       were different somehow, sadder but softer,
the mother pressing her cheek to the child's,
       certain she will lose him forever.
Still, her gaze does not waiver,
        his waif-like body rising to meet
          her heavy bent face,
his tiny hand, just visible, closing around her neck.

That night, waiting for sleep's elusive gesture
to turn the projector of my body inward
      I dreamt that Peter was with me,
not body touching body but rather
          a barely tangible hovering,
    the connection laboring to prove itself,
the morning's lecture still in my ears,
       operatic in its unfolding.

Long/Island/City

Birds disobey all human guidelines;
even though the signs advise,
                    do not touch,
as the fountains gather and
                    re-gather water
they thrust their tiny wings downward
                    over and over
in the imitation of flight. Hungry things
with dry mouths, they bow and dive,
threaten to come inside, eyeing
            the statues, their possible nests.
One can only hope there is no oil in their hands.

Inside, the light beats leaves into the floor,
it splays its futile body everywhere.
Nuguchi meant to re-invent it,
        in this space that is
                half-building, half-air
opening up into a garden of Japanese trees.
The granite is altered so slightly
                it seems almost untouched,
rather, merely an object holding the room down,
asking us to look away from the secular,
            this man-made landscape
offering up its one reprieve,
its one moment of stillness.

Nothing to Be Gained Here

When we arrived at the painter's last studio
we did not expect to see the door
wide open to the street as if it
were somehow waiting for us.
It was not the sacred space I'd hoped for
but only a work place,
a building like all the others.
Still, I searched for some lingering fact,
any kind of proof, only to come up empty,
as if blinded by my own looking.
I could have kissed you right then
but instead turned to examine the bathroom window,
the supposedly cracked pane
where he had written the words *broken-hearted*. But now
this too was gone and I called down to Tracy
waiting, perched on the stoop
like a Buddha, more patient
with my whims than ever.
The three of us drifted back
into the neighborhood of lamp shops
offering up their intimate light.
You pointed toward the wall where he
had left his own epitaph—*I am the best artist.*
It was telling how the irony
was wasted on you, the words,
like your gesture, now barely visible
through the dark.

Whose Music Excels the Music of Birds

The news of her death came to me late
as if from a messenger who, lost in his wandering,
    forgets all text.
You broke it to me over the phone at work
during one of our fights,
    our shameless meanderings
as to whether we did or did not love each other,
   the fact a lingering ammunition,
a second kind of ending that day.
  I was trapped in the moment—
a toss-up between the brutality of movement
   and the impossibility of stillness—
the suddenly malevolent Christmas shoppers
    a swarm of glowing distractions,
the noise of their footsteps and chatter
a seemingly *violent music.* It disturbed them,
   this dangerous experiment against composure,
    a girl running past
in the too obvious display of grief.

Complete in my autobiography of dirty feathers
   I fled to the exit,
    beating wings inside out,
toward the snow I somehow knew
was beginning for the first time that winter
   to collect on the statues,
the art trying to fend off its white heaviness.

I sat down in it as if attempting
        through my own body
                to imprint the cold record of hers.
I remembered the footage of a young poet
in cat-eye glasses describing her Peggy Guggenheim Foundation
                washer and dryer,
hands twisted downward full of smoke
                        with a room full of casual onlookers
watching as she sat at her typewriter composing a music that
                excels the music of birds;
        a language not able to make
the usual distinction
        between the words and the singing.

Widener Library

Across the table your hand raises like a flag,
   falls, fluttering,
into mine rising to meet it, as we
     move through the ellipsis
       the empty pause,
toward this, our necessary gesture. We are like poets
trying to sell words to each other.

Now, we sit on the stairs of the library with all the rest
    waiting for it to begin,
one poet reading the work of another,
    translating a similar language
into her own sweet vernacular, her own breathy beckoning.
She is not quite what a poet should be
   but something slightly less wild,
trapped in her own iconography, her own history of telling.
Here, even the grass is academic,
    the nonchalant cumulous clouds reflected over,
eyeing the crowd like *mad nightingales.*
It is as though someone has asked her to explain the words
   but instead she insists
     on the weight, the pause,
as we are told to recognize not the language but
     the spaces in between.

Unfortunately, bit by bit, I am beginning to forget you
                even as you are here, directly before me
tilted onto the stone stair, soaking up all the light. Even
as I think of you and sometimes get caught up in this thinking
as if my thoughts were a trail of film left in the projector,
    spinning endlessly.
What is being in love anyway but a complete misunderstanding—
                  an untrue image superimposed over
                  the body of the other.
But, then again, sometimes there is no end to longing.
Both poets know this, the one who reads and the one being read.
I try to concentrate on the movement,
                the insistent lyric but rather I
am thinking of how, moments earlier, I had asked
you to leave me in this life, if only,
                as we both like to say, for now.
When I look over at you, you no longer exist—
                    only the implication of.

Utopia(n) Parkway

She liked to measure things by their approximate distance
    to/from other things:
the fact that it took the tow truck 37 blocks to arrive,
the way the proportions of his body differed from hers,
how this might affect motion. Thus, what seemed
hours to her, to him was merely minutes.

Or, the distance from her to him at any given moment
on any given day. We could call it
the usual lull of marriage,
we could call it the documentation of
the conversation as poetics. It all started when they found
drug paraphernalia in the armrest between the seats,
from there it was all downhill. The radio play did not help
the situation, interrupted, as usual, before the conclusion.

Knowing that he was tired of her ability to take any situation
and make the worst of it. She tried to talk it up, saying,
*At least we didn't blow out on the bridge. At least we're in a safe
neighborhood. At least it's warm and we're together.*

If she did measure things by their approximation to other things
she might have chosen to call this story, the story of the car,
a story about Joseph Cornell's house.
Jo Cornell's brother had it too,
only then it was called being an invalid or
in valid.

The Music Of:

John, Once Again I Fall into the Realm of Utter Peril

The body has its own form of chaos, a solar system
through which it moves. When you touch me you
become a smaller part of this balance and it is
unclear whether it is skin or the idea of skin you are
reaching for. When I shake I can feel your temptation
to wound me, to tack me down like a saved, dead
insect. If my spine were not a question mark. If my
hands were not flutters.

Six Mutilations to the Body

The one who floods the private sanctuary I've built,
who takes away sleep,
who drags and throws me under,
that presence is the joy I speak of.

—Rumi

One: Social problems are the effects of men's ideas
about themselves.

I go with you to get your first pierce. It concerns a
needle and cork, a man with a fat stomach and dusty
hands. He carries tattoos from wrist to upper arm to
back. They are meaningless to your eyes glazed in
pain. The room is dark with dirty walls. It smells like
nervousness, blood, or urine. The man takes your
penis between fingers while you struggle to keep it
limp and I, not being your girlfriend, avert my eyes
but keep your palm. When the needle strikes your
head you don't flinch, only grasp my hand tighter.

Two: There is no point in lamenting the world.

Your waist is always getting thinner. I can almost put
two fingers around your body. We go dancing and
you are the one who wants to leave early. It chases
us, this disease that tears men down like crumbling
cities. A person is a person, a pile of sticks, then
nothing. We are a box of what ifs. It seems as though
there should be a way to get back but our disease,
your disease, is not like that. It gets larger everyday,
then smaller.

Three: Love the world as your own self, then you can
      truly care for all things.

Are you a sadist or a masochist, that's what I want
to know. It took you hours to twist the wire hanger
into the exact configuration, your hands marked and
bleeding. *I want to have a brand to see what it will be
like when I.* Although you don't finish, I know what
you mean. You heat the wire over the gas stove like a
junkie. I beg you to come out. *No, I don't want to go
for coffee. I can't tell you any more secrets, you know
too many of them by heart already. Be surprised if
I even ever leave this house again.* This dark room
with the water-worn ceiling. You press the wire to
your arm. For weeks I find scabs around your house
like bread crumbs falling in your footsteps.

Four: I am not this fragile body.

You tell us a story, your brother and I, about shooting
up LSD, a drug meant to be swallowed like candy,
not shoved into veins. You spit balls of green and blue
phlegm. I never did go to the place where you were
born, with its tree-lined streets and rain. If I had I
might have been the one to hold the tourniquet for
you with shaking hands. You would have done the
same for me. I, too, might have shared this disease
you hold so deeply in your body, the one you guard.
Yet, I know you after the drugs have dissipated,
leaving only these stories.

Five: Love is the effective path.

Get it straight, you tell me, *get it straight. We are
not lovers. Your love for me, like theater, looks three
dimensional but only has two. Get it straight. Love for
you is flat, like the earth, like the desert that surrounds
us.* I say you've been reading too many books, your
mind is lost in metaphors. I say, I hear you. I can hear
you because you are whispering in my ear. I hear you
but I won't listen. I don't need to be told I don't exist.
It's already evident in my eyes.

Six: Death is the opposite of time.

If there were a drug for me it would be your skin or
the history of it. I am attracted to your swollen arms.
Perhaps I love them because they are bloated and
will never be able to hold me. Maybe I want you to
die but if I did I would ask that death be fast and
leave little mark. I would go down all at once like
falling down stairs instead of disintegrating with
you, one step at a time.

All that Is Solid Melts into Air

For example, all fleeing birds. Geese, when high enough,
disappear into the gray, the kind arrows of their bodies
keeping them in sync. Like them, when absent from the
text of my body, I am able to propel myself in a form
of movement faster and easier than I'd imagined. This
morning a blue jay appeared on the porch railing, fanning
his particular crowned head, waiting for his mate. Somehow
my dreams were part of this equation. It is not my fault that
I have always considered starlings to be ugly, their chatter
filling the day like monks at dinner taking a break from the
endless work of silence. Yet my previous theory proves itself
untrue. I can still see the geese craning their necks forward
in the undetermined gesture of leaving or coming back.

The Music Of:

Our two versions of the same story are different. This is
because you are my darling. For me the cello could easily be
considered the personification of desperation. For you it is
an act of romance. As is the case with all missing lovers, you
count the days systematically, excluding the ones which serve
as mere distractions. You claim that you had loved more on
this day than all the others combined. Does it not follow then
that our bodies are capable of composing themselves? Does it
not follow then that this body might not be what I wanted in a
particular moment, a lullaby?

Walking the Park with Joseph

If I try to forget anything it will be your hands. The way you
sit with one leg wrapped around another. You are a house
of candles, a place that all monks like to visit. You are a
Chinese wife with long black hair and a dying child. You
told me about her skirt, how it fell about her waist. How you
dreamt of her and woke empty. I am detached, detached
all the time, shining like rings of coffee on sheets of notes.
All of the time smiling like the statues in a Paris museum,
not the Louvre but the one I've never been to. You say,
please don't go. The walk is too long. It is too cold.
And besides, words once written lose their music.

Misnomer

Dear mother. Dear girl.

You have smothered me. From birth your body stole the
air from my skin, making it formless. You were my savior
and destroyer in these early moments from what little
I remember of the event. It is said that those who remember
their own births are liars.

Your body was composed of walls. At times it is as though
I did not give birth to you, as though you were a found
object. I meant to tell you what happened that day,
I meant to rewrite it.

I am all stumbles, all bones. When I stepped onto the
subway people turned as though checking experience
against their own expectation. I wanted to tell them how
I am trapped, for me the corporeal is a box. My limbs
are almost worthless, never doing exactly as I ask them.
When I speak it's as though speaking though water.

Or, it is as though your birth did not occur at all. The doctor
offered not to resuscitate you. He told me to pretend it did
not happen and start all over again. My body would not
take you back, my womb would not reform you.

In dreams I touch your limbs and know that they are tired.
That you have been worn, as I have been worn. Hang your
head for me when you say your prayers at night, don't let
the last one slip.

This morning I saw a crippled girl out of my window;
she was the only one on the street dancing.

Poem For Elizabeth #3

I.

My father wanted to rest in his usual kind of sickness, meaning:
rather than do the task at hand, be it social or otherwise, he
would prefer to read. My father is a champion reader, one who
is vast and non-discriminate in his undertaking, and can do
it for hours. So, when he wanted to stay in the motel room we
were, needless to say, disappointed but not surprised.

II.

Sometimes objects surpass their intended significance.
Therefore, the motel right off the highway no longer serves
as mere practicality, but something that has new meaning in
her absence. The absence reconfigures space—or at least his
version thereof. It is never the actual thing that changes but
the story we insist upon assigning it.

III.

So, my sister Marisa, my step-mother Elizabeth, and I decided
to go into The City without him. Although BART seemed to
bother neither Marisa nor Elizabeth, I have always found
something eerie about going under the ocean. Taking the
train means traveling into a new weather. When we reached
the other side, it was as though the sun had never existed,
riding into a canopy of clouds.

IV.

For him, her body created an outline, a map to navigate by.
In this, The City was no longer a singular place but a series
of representations. Everything must be reassigned then.
Everything must be redescribed by a new form of light.
In lieu of this, he will choose temporary blindness.

V.

What I remember most about Elizabeth is that she liked bags. My father says that this may have come from the fact that when she was little she visited her aunt in New York City every summer. In New York shopkeepers are famous for creating garbage, bags within bags within bags. On our trip, it was Elizabeth who wanted to stop at the department store on the way to the museum.

VI.

"Until that time, I had understood death as something entirely separate from and independent of life. The hand of death is bound together to take us, I felt, but until the day it reaches out for us it leaves us alone. This had seemed to me the simple, logical truth. Life is here, death over there. I am here, not over there."

—Haruki Murakami

VII.

While buying anything practical was out of the question, we knew it was the bag she was after; not the object itself but its mere representation. We made our way up to the sales floor to the rows of dishes. She knew exactly how to make sense of these random things, how to find an alphabet to them. We waited, seemingly forever, until she found just the right thing. At the time seemed like a meaningless errand.

VIII.

Marisa may not remember this day, she may remember a different one or none at all. Alternately, she may remember the day and think it nothing special about it. There is no telling how the memory will later piece things together, what it will or will not choose to make significant.

IX.

For now, the two landscapes they inhabited will remain illegible.

The Irony of Swans
for rachel

A fence entangles the park inventing a shelter for nature or
longing. We came here last summer to hear Bach with your
friend who is a poet and your friend who is gentle. The woman
behind us drank too much, her laughter creating interludes
both annoying and contagious, the wine corks making the
tiny pops of frogs in the wilderness. She was a child prodigy
until her body built this resistance to music. Walking home
we linked arms like we tend to do, meaning everything and
nothing by it.

Now, it is just your mother, John, and I. John and I holding
hands in a more complicated gesture. Your mother is telling
a story of how your sister fell in the icy water, how she tried
to grab her and missed at the last moment, how your sister's
bones clamored against each other, her skin trying to separate
itself from the wet winter clothes. And we know it is like this,
your mother always grasping and always just missing. Your
sister insisting that they continue the walk to the museum.
Your sister always looking toward art for warmth.

Hypnagogic Diary

Hypnagogic Diary

> *You must fall asleep before the birds begin*
> *or there's no hope for it.*
>> *for jim campbell*

Alone, waiting for the light
to turn in its particular language
the plastic dime-store stars
come out one by one, an occasional
cloud drifting over. In this
white screen refrain
the mind reiterates what the body
thought it had forgotten;
such as, *when one moves too quickly*
the soul is left behind. Such as,
I have moved too quickly. Or,
bells swing in an airless room
without any hand reaching up to touch them.

The night holds itself in fits and starts.
I imagine all the possibilities,
all the ways it could go down. That night
we moved around the darkening pond
with all the others, the lanterns reflected
in water making the light
more than it intended to be.
You drifted along the edge
waiting to be caught up. What is it
about her that makes her
such an objective; *dear you,*
always needing to know
the definition of lyrical.

At the last moment something like a moan
stops you, as if
it were the soul's insistence on
saving you the trouble of it all.
Sleep is not a reprieve
but rather a tunnel
that returns you to longing
much in the way the slow light
comes into the room
redescribing the objects
one by one: a list of words
pasted to the kitchen wall,
your various icons,
a photograph of your brother
his sweetest image.

In the restaurant a myriad
dusty ceramic saints look
down upon us, seemingly moved
to pity, each holding court
on their separate altars
like a museum for the holy.
I try to find solace
in the relentless salsa music.
Sometimes what we think of
as an awkward pause
is merely silence trying
to prove its own accuracy.
Or, what I meant to tell you was
no one is stealing anyone
from anyone else.

With no hope for return
I stay on the seemingly
harmless periphery
without the threat or comfort of
falling. The mind wants to linger here
as thoughts lift and clamor
interrupting the room's stillest landscape.
A few houses away
you are also not sleeping
but rather making
an insomniac film
of your own—a plotless story
that you insist upon believing.
As you peer through her
Magritte painting of a body
you do not see my words
filling the sky with explanation
rather a series of perfect
images veiling the light. You know
I am a failure in this body
with no regard for silence
or objects.

Two people speak inside
this space held in darkness, *a kind of*
unlistening, a kind unlistening.
What he means to say is lost,
obscured by sleep's strange
vernacular. She will wait
until morning to decipher,
to sort the thing out. Outside
she can hear the cars
rushing toward their own
variation on reality, knowing
that one way to find beauty is
in the absence of it.

In the next room, before light-
fall, you move about
with your familiar tick
of silver against glass.
The sound of the water,
constant in its drifting,
lulls me back
into some kind of ritual where
things mean to stand for other things.
As I rise to the surface
I realize these are not your gestures
but those of another
that hold me, keep me in place
proving the unconscious—
in order to make itself comfortable—
will pull any series of tricks.
Before, in the dream, there were flowers
like an arrangement of signs.

Now, you are no longer yourself
but a variation of.
I resist taking you in,
not in repulsion but worry.
You prove your accidental cruelty
in this structure that can
no longer bother to move
beyond itself, redefining our
ideal, our own small interest
in death. When you go
will you leave behind merely
a space that the human figure once filled
or will a likeness remain?
As mundane as it sounds,
I am finally settling into this life.